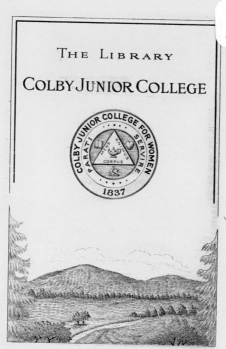

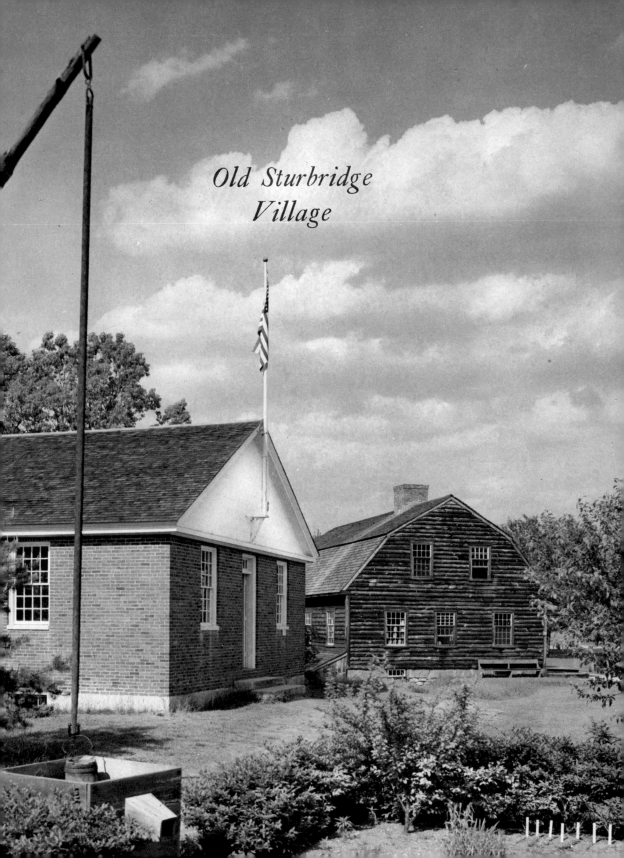

Old Sturbridge Village

THE VILLAGE MEETING HOUSE

Old Sturbridge Village

A Photographic Impression by

SAMUEL CHAMBERLAIN

HASTINGS HOUSE, *Publishers* NEW YORK 22

Miner Grant's Store

Wight's Grist Mill

FOREWORD

If rain had not fallen on a certain Saturday afternoon about a quarter of a century ago, thus spoiling a golf foursome, it is quite possible that this book about a remarkable village would never have been written. On that particular day Mr. Albert B. Wells was persuaded by his friends to join them in an antique hunt as a substitute for the rained-out game of golf. Local history does not record who bought the most antiques that day, but there is no doubt of the eventual winner in the afternoon's sport. It was Mr. Wells — and the American public. The collecting virus seized him instantly. Although he had long been interested in early handicrafts, the acquisitive urge had not flowered to any great extent. Now began the exhilarating adventure of collecting. Mr. Wells threw himself into it with what appears to be joyous abandon. From farmhouse attics, barns, mills, country stores, and early workshops he gathered old tools, furniture, glass, and a hundred different oddities which recalled the American way of life before the industrial revolution. Mr. Wells was a part of that revolution, being a reigning power in the highly efficient American Optical Company, in nearby Southbridge. Yet the homely crafts of his ancestors held a greater fascination for him. His younger brother, J. Cheney Wells, was also becoming a collector, but with more specific hobbies — particularly early American clocks and glass paper weights.

The combined Wells collections soon mushroomed into a storage problem. Antiques poured into the large Albert Wells house, filling the attic and intruding upon the basement bowling alley, to the consternation of the younger Wells children. The pressure of new acquisitions was relentless, and soon the family found themselves moving out of the house and converting it into an Historical Museum. But this was only a momentary solution for displaying what was now a most significant collection. Then the idea of Old Sturbridge Village, a living community dramatizing the early New England way of life, burst forth as a radiant answer to the problem. A few short years have proven that this was an inspired conception. The re-created New England village not only displays the amazing Wells collection of early objects, it brings the whole epoch back to life.

To activate such a village, Mr. Wells began to collect whole houses, stores and barns, and to move them to a pleasant site near the Quinebaug River. Here they were re-assembled to typify a New England settlement in the early 1800's. To round out the picture, some new structures were built along old lines, a grist mill and a blacksmith's shop were rebuilt, a sawmill was moved from Connecticut, and a Village Meeting House was transported from nearby Fiskdale to its proud place at the end of the Green. Old Sturbridge Village is still in an active and healthy state of growth. A mansion from Charlton will soon take its place near the other end of the Green. An old farm is even now being re-assembled. Constant changes are being made to facilitate matters for visitors, who now find two agreeable lunching places and good over-night accommodations in the historic Oliver Wight House and in a neighboring group of guest houses. More changes are in view, and it should be emphasized that this book shows only the village of today.

They used to say that you could reach Old Sturbridge Village from the outskirts of New York City by taking the Connecticut parkways and turning left at the first traffic light, (toll stations excluded). This was literally true if you chose the broad new parkways across Connecticut and drove some six miles into lower Massachusetts. But now a colossal clover leaf has supplanted the traffic light, and the facile phrase is no longer strictly accurate. But the Village is accessible and easy to find, being located in mid-Massachusetts near the intersection of three important roads. It lies just off the main highway between Boston and New York. Providence, Hartford, Springfield, and Worcester are within convenient driving distance.

With the physical growth of the Village came the development of its educational mission and its vitality as a living community. Its sponsors sought primarily to create a convincing background against which to dramatize the skill, ingenuity, and thrift of the early New Englander. They did not attempt to re-create an actual town, nor to insist upon rigid authenticity down to the last brick, clapboard, and hand-made nail. The Village of today is neither a museum nor a minutely accurate restoration, but something far more fascinating to the public —

an animated, functioning community. A miller is grinding corn in the old grist mill as you pass by. Beyond him the village blacksmith is hammering away at his anvil and a cabinet maker is putting the finishing touches on a drop-leaf table. You are free to wander about and watch the potter working at his wheel or kiln, to observe the intricate arts of the coppersmith and the weaver, or to see the chips fly as the wood worker fashions a mahogany salad bowl. What is more, you may purchase the very articles you see being made, for these are self-supporting artisans. Finally, they will answer your questions, and without a trace of weariness in their voices. In view of all this, the popularity of the crafts program is not suprising. It is difficult to overstate its educational value. The number of school groups making annual pilgrimages is increasing by leaps and bounds, for the Village holds an absolute fascination for children. Education couldn't come in a more pleasant form.

From its inception this living demonstration of early New England life and crafts has been the heartbeat of Old Sturbridge Village, but there are many individuals who, in the wake of the Wells brothers, have contributed mightily to its vitality. First among these is Mrs. Ruth Dyer Wells, a lady whose buoyant enthusiasm is a phenomenon to behold. Her responsibility is now shared by an able and imaginative staff, two members of which were particularly kind and helpful to me in preparing this book. To Mr. Earle W. Newton, the Director, to Mr. Frank O. Spinney, the Curator, and to the ebullient Mrs. Wells I beg to express ardent and heartfelt thanks.

This book has a modest objective — to give at least an *impression* of the charm of Old Sturbridge Village, a hint of its varied collections, and a glimpse of its highly praised crafts program. While this does not aspire to be a factual guidebook, the pictures do follow a logical sequence. They begin with the historic Oliver Wight House and follow the natural footpath which a visitor might take. I hope that this fact qualifies it to serve as a discreet but talkative companion at the reader's elbow, and later to act as a retrospective reminder of this extraordinary village, beyond a doubt the antiquarian event of this quarter-century in New England — the one which began on a rainy, golfless Saturday afternoon.

SAMUEL CHAMBERLAIN

THE OLIVER WIGHT HOUSE

Old Sturbridge Village lies close to the Old Bay Path of pioneer days, and to the modern highway now known to motorists as Route 20. To generations of travelers on the historic road, the most imposing landmark along the way has been this cheerful square mansion which rejoices in so many 24-paned windows. Today's visitor will probably glimpse it first among the Village properties, and it is notably easy to gaze upon. Architects are intrigued by its four doorways, all of them well designed, and by its exceedingly rare combination of hip and gambrel roofs. It follows the conventional two-chimney, central hallway plan in other respects.

The house has served in its time as an administration building, but its large and gracious rooms are now reconverted into overnight accommodations for visitors to Old Sturbridge Village.

The south doorway has a subtle nine-panelled portal.

The Oliver Wight House, silhouetted against the earliest buds of spring. The house was built in 1783, by Oliver Wight, son of David Wight, Sr., who had bought a thousand acres of this rather desolate land ten years before. Oliver Wight may have been another Mr. Blandings in his time, for he apparently squandered himself out of house and home, and was soon forced to sell his mansion to an innkeeper, Ebenezer Howard. Oliver's brother, David Wight Jr. had better luck. Once while making a business trip to Boston in 1786, young David dug into his savings and risked ten dollars on a ticket in the Harvard College lottery. A year later his ticket won a prize of $5,000, a bounty which enabled him to buy a large parcel of land and to build an even more impressive mansion nearby. But, sadly enough, it burned to the ground in 1926. Ebenezer Howard, the innkeeper, was also a cabinet maker of sorts. When a guest in the house fell mortally ill, Ebenezer was asked to build the coffin. His charges were so outrageous, however, that the dead man's relatives complained to the Selectmen, who promptly deprived the innkeeper of his license. But the inn was too popular to remain closed for any length of time, and Ebenezer soon found a relative in whose name the license was granted.

The Oliver Wight House in contrasting seasons. Pale winter sunlight brings out the peculiar roof construction of the house, its unsymmetrical east façade and, above all, the noble architecture of the elms.

The midsummer majesty of this trio of elms overshadows the Oliver Wight House and its venerable red barn. The property became a part of Old Sturbridge Village in 1936.

The broad central hallway of the Oliver Wight House is furnished with antiques and reproductions from the Village Cabinet Shop. Its wide front door is sternly plain, but the walls are animated with frescoes painted in 1832, by that most celebrated of itinerant wall painters, Rufus Porter.

The Rufus Porter frescoes are toned a soft grey-green. The migratory artist alternated stencils with free-hand brush work to achieve his decorative effect. Recently the frescoes have been restored.

From the quiet banks of the Quinebaug River you get a first glimpse of the Village. Only the spire of the Village Meeting House stands out clearly, casting a thin, wavering reflection in the river.

The placid river suddenly becomes forceful as it spills over a dam and rushes under the old bridge. You will soon be walking over the foot bridge dimly discernible, at the right.

CHENEY SAW-MILL

At the eastern extremity of the Mill Pond, where old David Wight had built a saw-mill in post-Revolutionary days, now stands a venerable L-shaped replacement which once flourished in Gilead, Connecticut. Lumber was a vital commodity in any early settlement, and saw-mills such as this were usually its first commercial enterprise. This type of mill is noteworthy for its vertical "up-and-down" saw, which is operated by a water wheel. An ingenious mechanism moves the saw up and down and simultaneously draws the log forward. The advent of the circular saw forced the older system into obsolescence, but it could not erase evidence of Yankee skill and inventiveness. This weathered mill is a forceful reminder of the fact.

The Mill Pond on a summer day.

The mill pond flows under this galleried wing of the Cheney saw-mill. Underneath the building is a primitive turbine or "flutter" wheel which revolved horizontally as the water rushed past its blades.

The working organism of the water-driven vertical saw can be studied here by the mechanically minded. The Cheney saw-mill was moved to this spot and re-erected in 1936.

THE WIGHT GRIST MILL combines essential utility with a charming picturesqueness. The latter quality is more evident in this spring-time vista across the narrow mill stream.

THE WIGHT GRIST MILL

According to the local historians, the site of David Wight's first mill was discovered by the Wight boys when they tracked a cow through the thicket and down to the water's edge. Here they observed that the river overflowed at one point. Their father built a dam at this strategic spot along the Quinebaug River, and set up a water power system which was used by his family for three generations. The Wight mills have long since disappeared, but this reconstruction of a typical grist mill is on David Wight's original location. The machinery was moved from the old Porter Grist Mill at Hebron, Connecticut, in 1938.

The impressive 20-foot water wheel revolves silently around its stone-supported pivot. This is an "under-shot" wheel, the water flowing under the road and striking the blades near the bottom of the wheel with enough force to turn it steadily.

In winter the spokes of the old water wheel carry a shimmering glace of ice.

The interior of the Wight Grist Mill is an atmospheric place where yellow and white corn meal, whole wheat, graham, rye, and buckwheat flour are ground between 18th century burr stones, and sold to epicurean visitors.

Discarded mill stones form a part of the Wight Grist Mill display. They are immense, flat and round, with sharp grooves cut in their faces. This midsummer view also shows the Cheney Saw-mill.

The miller who officiates at the Wight Grist Mill lives behind a picket fence in a gambrel-roofed cottage reminiscent of Cape Cod.

Beyond the spindly silhouettes of aging buckboards stands the BLACKSMITH'S HOUSE, a smiling pitch-roofed cottage copied from one, which once stood on the Wight property. The windows are spaced with true, rugged New England individualism.

The boarded, whitewashed walls of the Blacksmith's House are well adapted to display Mr. Albert B. Wells' collection of early wrought iron, some of which obviously comes from the Iberian peninsula.

There are endless ways of opening the front door of a New England house, and the Wells collection of iron latches and handles proves it. Many of these pieces are reproduced in the Blacksmith Shop.

STONE BLACKSMITH SHOP

This nostalgic structure is a copy of the George Stone blacksmith shop which stood at Gilmanton Ironworks, New Hampshire. It is crammed to the rafters with an atmospheric miscellany, including the sort of sleigh your grandparents used to ride in. Silhouetted against the window at the left is an ox-break, a sturdy device for shoeing oxen, which comes from Brimfield, Massachusetts. Unlike a horse, an ox cannot stand on three legs, nor does he have the same forbearance for blacksmiths. Consequently he had to be cajoled or forced into the ox-break enclosure. Then a leather sling was fastened under his belly and he was lifted in the air. After attaching his hooves with four leather loops, the blacksmith was ready to go to work — accompanied by belligerent bellowing. The present day smithy engages also in the milder pursuit of reproducing domestic iron hardware at his anvil.

The shop of this village blacksmith stands under a mighty tree, true enough, but contrary to poetic tradition, it happens to be not a chestnut but an elm.

Surrounding the shop of the smithy was a traditional graveyard of discarded vehicles, a detail which has not been overlooked in the Stone Blacksmith Shop. Under the elm is a water trough, hewn from a log.

A wide overhang shelters the east façade of the Blacksmith Shop. In the foreground is a round tire-setting stone, on which the blacksmith placed the wooden wagon wheel before fitting it with a red hot iron tire.

The picturesque vehicles of early New Englanders, from buckboards to barouches, are displayed in the open-air wagon shed which adjoins the Stone Blacksmith Shop. Antique birdhouses perch on the rafters.

A sleigh, a sulky, and a Tally-ho are among the retired veterans in the wagon shed. The side walls are enlivened with a display of old iron hinges, chains, and pot hooks.

The entrance hall of the Village Tavern has a cheerful dignity, enhanced by the presence of a handsome clock from the J. Cheney Wells collection. The wallpaper repeats a favorite New England design.

The reception room at the Village Tavern has much of the atmosphere of a village ballroom, for the instruments and music racks of a country orchestra are set up in place, ready for the first waltz.

The game room of the Village Tavern is carpeted with simple rugs and furnished with sturdy, unpretentious early American chairs and tables, well suited to checker players, clay pipe smokers, and ale drinkers.

The game room affords an opportunity to display a small part of the Wells collection of pewter. Many rooms are devoted to collections, the most notable being an extraordinary group of lighting devices.

The Great Room is roofed with massive arched beams which came from a venerable house in Mashapaug, Connecticut. Down the center of the room runs a butcher's table notched with a central channel for running off the blood. The wing chairs are solidly panelled, to keep out the drafts on cold winter nights.

One needs a better word than "huge" or "massive" to describe the stone fireplace of the Great Room. It is so big it actually has a window. The chimney occupies as much space as a large room.

Adjoining the bar, just off the Great Room, is a rustic staircase of great solidity. Its steps are solid blocks of wood, the upper ones being hewn away, triangular-wise. The bar is embellished with an appropriate collection of old bottles, decanters, demijohns, and drinking glasses.

The Buttery adjoins the Old Kitchen at the far end of the Great Room. Here are displayed the churns, strainers, baskets, bowls, and tubs used by the hardy New England housewife to make her butter and cheese.

The Old Kitchen is one of the most successful rooms in the Village Tavern. Its unconventional fireplace is fitted with an angular brick oven, a pivoted drying rack, and a fine choice of pots, trivets, and spiders.

Weathered vertical sheathing covers three of the walls of the Old Kitchen, but solid stone frames the husky soapstone sink. The room pays a notable tribute to the use of wood — in utensils, furniture, and construction.

One of the rooms in the Village Tavern is furnished as an 18th century visitor might have found it —
except for the tell-tale base plug.

Small chests were much more a hobby of our ancestors than they are with us, to judge by this diversified
exhibit in the Village Tavern. Some of the chests open up into writing desks.

This chill view of the Common was taken from the porch of the Tavern. The silhouette of the SOLOMON RICHARDSON HOUSE and the dim form of the Meeting House are framed in the columns.

Summer cloaks the old salt-box in quite a different atmosphere. The village pump and its massive granite trough stand in the front of the Gebhard Barn, as does this lovely old vehicle, which seems to cry out for a horse and a sentimental young couple.

The Solomon
Richardson House
in contrasting sea-
sons of winter and
spring.

THE SOLOMON RICHARDSON HOUSE

By far the most engaging spot of color on the Village Green is this red-and-white salt-box house at lilac time. It has another distinction, for it was actually built in a town called Podunk, near East Brookfield, Massachusetts. A Housewright by the name of Thomas Bannister chose Podunk as the place to exhibit his professional skill, somewhere around 1748. Probably he was a speculative builder, for he sold the house to Solomon Richardson, a carpenter, about a year later. The present façade is fairly dressy for such an old house, and one surmises that carpenter Richardson, or maybe one of his sons, added the white front doorway with its rich mouldings at a much later date. The house relinquished its Podunk post-office address in 1940, when it was moved to this tranquil setting on the Village Green.

Front doorway of the Solomon Richardson House.

The long back room under the sloping roof of the Solomon Richardson House is arranged as an exhibition space for early American furniture.

Under the handsome four-poster in the west bedroom is a rope-spring trundle bed.

Neat panelling of subtly varying width frames the living room fireplace.

The very essence of Colonial times is distilled in the front hallway of the Solomon Richardson House. It is the prototype of hundreds throughout New England. The stair rail is the original one built by Thomas Bannister, although the delicately feathered vertical sheathing is a restoration.

When the Solomon Richardson House was moved from Podunk, nothing remained of the original central chimney. This wide rear fireplace, modelled after a 17th century Essex County type, was completed in 1940.

This atmospheric corner of the back room is enlivened by a writing-arm Windsor chair, a raised blanket chest with a slanting lid, a pewter shelf, a spinning wheel, and a highly decorative hobby horse.

THE MASHAPAUG HOUSE

This simple pitched-roof cottage, whose façade shows such charming disregard for symmetry and whose general atmosphere is so reminiscent of the late 17th century, is one of the more recent veterans to be transplanted to the Village Green. It was once a salt-box also, to judge by its plunging roof line, but a long 18th century ell has largely nullified the salt-box silhouette. Traces of faded red paint still linger on the clapboards.

This informal backyard view shows the rear wing and the woodshed of the Mashapaug House, the latter manifesting a hospitable interest in pigeons.

The brook, which runs under the woodshed of the Mashapaug House, is disciplined by a stone enclosure and a rail fence. The house serves as a town library and also holds the Village's reference collection.

An ell is usually an afterthought, brought on by a growing family roster, but it has its picturesque virtues. This full length view of the Mashapaug House should prove the point.

The focal point in the large front room in the Mashapaug House is this broad fireplace, framed in time-stained panels.

There is a Whittieresque quality to this view of Old Sturbridge Village, taken in the pale sunlight of a March morning. The snow-powdered road curves around the Mashapaug House and passes the church.

THE VILLAGE MEETING HOUSE, standing serenely at the head of Old Sturbridge Village Common, serves as a symbol of the spiritual heritage of New England, and as a functioning undenominational church.

THE VILLAGE MEETING HOUSE

The Village Green and the houses we have just visited stretch out below the simple white church and its sheltering elm. Before being moved to this reposeful slope the old church had stood for more than a century in the neighboring town of Fiskdale. Originally built in Sturbridge Center in 1832, by a Baptist Society which traces its beginnings back to 1747, it was moved two miles to Fiskdale in 1838. There it served as the Fiskdale Baptist Church for many years until it was given to Old Sturbridge Village. On May 15th, 1949, after moving and extensive restoration, it was rededicated on this spot, where its simple dignity will be preserved for future generations. Its architecture is far simpler than the Christopher Wren-inspired examples so current in New England, but it has a grace and a certain restrained integrity which typifies New England best of all.

The severity of the ceiling of the Village Meeting House is broken by three handsome early American candelabra.

The interior is restored as it was originally built, with galleries on three sides and four rows of enclosed rectangular pews. The panelling is notably good.

Early spring near the Village Meeting House.

The most recent addition to the family of old structures on the Village Green is the FENNO HOUSE, a two-story dwelling with a lean-to, originally built by John Fenno at Canton, Massachusetts in 1704.

THE STEPHEN FITCH HOUSE

The next oldest house in this assembled community is a weathered, unpretentious dwelling which was originally built in Windham, Connecticut, now a part of Willimantic. It demonstrates dramatically how a New England house grows. Stephen Fitch, of Coventry, took his young bride to settle uninhabited acres in the wilds of Windham, and first built a one-room cabin whose exposed gunstock corner posts are still visible. This was in 1735. To the cabin subsequently were added a husky stone chimney and another room with sensitive pine paneling. This may have been built for the Fitch's son Jesse and *his* bride.

The roof was raised to permit upstairs rooms, and it was extended to the rear, to shelter a newly built "long kitchen" and an adjoining kitchen chamber. By the dawn of the 19th century, the Fitch family had multiplied considerably and a kitchen ell was added somewhere between 1800 and 1820.

The Frog Pond, directly behind the Stephen Fitch house, adds a musical note to Old Sturbridge Village.

The façade of the Stephen Fitch House is faced with deep-cut, unpainted pine clapboards, copied from the Windham originals. Double-sash windows, "nines-over-sixes," had come into use by Fitch's time.

The Stephen Fitch House is rich in murky atmosphere on an overcast winter day. It possesses that comparative rarity, a "half-gambrel" roof, the roof line being broken in front, and straight behind.

The west living room of the Stephen Fitch House reflects a less pioneering way of life. The pine sheathing and panelling has a certain style, and the fireplace, spanned by a massive granite lintel, is framed in well-cut mouldings.

THE DENESON SCHOOLHOUSE

No small New England community would be complete without its "little red schoolhouse" with the American flag fluttering overhead. Old Sturbridge Village has a fine example in the replica of an old brick school located in the Deneson district of Southbridge. It was named for James Deneson, an early settler who was the first to clamor for town schools. Throughout the years the building has sheltered a variety of exhibits.

The furnishings of the west living room in the Stephen Fitch House reflect the dawn of the Georgian influence in America. At the left is a Queen Anne drop leaf table. The grandfather clock was made by the first clock maker in southern New Hampshire, Isaac Blaisdell, of Chester. He imported the elaborate dial from England.

The kitchen-bedroom provides a vista of the same west living room.

The "Grey Kitchen" was probably added as a rear wing shortly after 1800. Its Welch dresser is filled with old pewter, wooden plates, and wine bottles. On the wall hangs a baggy coat and a "Tricorne" hat.

The winter kitchen of the Stephen Fitch House provides a glimpse of two of the three fireplaces which are built into the massive stone chimney. In the foreground is the family table, set with wooden plates, knives and pewter spoons, but no forks, and surrounded with bow-back Windsor chairs.

The fireplace of the low-ceilinged "Grey Kitchen" has multiple ovens and over-mantle storage cupboards. It is not difficult to picture the Fitches and their assembled heirs around this pine table.

Here is the original downstairs room built by Stephen Fitch, with a slat-back rocker carefully placed before the fire for his bride. It pays eloquent tribute to his pioneer spirit and his ability as a craftsman.

MINER GRANT'S GENERAL STORE

This well-seasoned gambrel-roofed emporium began its career as the home of the Reverend John Willard, brother of President Joseph Willard of Harvard College. It was built in the village of Stafford Street, Connecticut, toward the end of the 18th century. The Reverend Willard used it for some years as a school to prepare young men for Harvard. In 1802 the house was bought by Miner Grant and converted into a country store. Being on the Hartford turnpike, it did a thriving business, and remained in the Grant family for 109 years. Later it was sold to Old Sturbridge Village and took its place as a trading post just off the Village Green in 1939. It now houses an extraordinary authentic and reminiscent conglomeration of old-time merchandise.

The village postoffice was a part of Miner Grant's country store, and it has been moved intact, together with an incredible miscellany, including parrot cages, coffee grinders, and the cello played by Clark Grant, son of the founder. Country dances were held in the second story ballroom of the store, and Clark Grant provided the music. He also kept the accounts, and his books are open for inspection on the bookkeeper's desk.

Miner Grant's General Store is built on a steep hillside. Here its weathered form is veiled by the earliest of spring foliage. In the distance is the Deneson Schoolhouse, shrouded in April buds.

The basement of the store is sheltered by a rustic porch and contains, among other things, a collection of stoves, iron utensils, and mechanical wooden apple-peelers.

Miner Grant's General Store looks particularly authentic in the setting of a New England winter. Its wet blackened shingles provide startling contrast to the melting snow. In the background are the Stephen Fitch House and the spire of the Meeting House.

In summer the front porch of the store offers two benches for the foot-weary, and the silent company of a wooden Indian, in the best cigar store tradition.

The stock of Miner Grant's Store is as varied as it is nostalgic. Baskets, hat boxes, carpet bags, bolts of patterned cottons and wooden scales are here, not to mention the classic cracker barrel.

The exposed wood stove, with its wire-suspended sheet-iron pipe, would seem to make Miner Grant's Store a poor fire hazard, but it has survived the risk for more than a century and a half. In its early days the store was essentially a trading post, and the storekeeper was obliged to barter imported "European and West Indian Goods" for farm products and local handicraft wares. The colonists had plenty of eggs, vegetables, and hay. In turn they needed powder, shot, calico, crockery, and glassware most among the European imports. From the West Indies they sought spices, molasses, indigo, sugar, and rum. Above all they needed salt. A successful shopkeeper had to be a masterful trader in those days!

All that is needed in this picture is a couple of old codgers playing checkers at this rustic board.

The pine shelves of Miner Grant's Store are filled with an astonishing mélange of articles that your rural grandparents used to buy, from horsewhips on the extreme left to hoopskirts on the extreme right. It must have been a joyous project to assemble this stock, which came partly from abandoned country stores.

A close-up of one of Miner Grant's shelves (opposite) reveals endless details of forgotten articles.

During the summer season a small selection of old-time candles, spices, and a few gifts are sold at this end of the store.

Other rooms in Miner Grant's Store are given over to such reminiscent exhibits as "Miss Smith's Dressmaking Shop" and to collections of domestic articles, such as these mortars, hand bells, and spice boxes.

A new and distinguished neighbor of Miner Grant's Store will be the OLD MANSION HOUSE which now sits on a knoll in nearby Charlton Village. This almost-square structure is the two-chimney type, with fine doorways and window trim, and a most unusual single-paned gallery above its hip roof.

Our path now leads away from the Village Green toward the two exhibition buildings shown at the right of this cloud-dominated picture. The taller structure with the brick chimney is the American Optical Building, a replica of the original factory which stood on Main Street in Southbridge. The small building discernible at the extreme right is the Tin Shop, a modest edifice whose whitewashed ground floor and attic contain an unexpected abundance of early tinware. Some of the pieces may seem a little routine, but not the grasshopper weathervane!

THE AMERICAN OPTICAL BUILDING

There are several exhibits of interest here, including this authentic reproduction of an early spectacle shop and watch mender's workroom. An extensive collection of glassware is shown in cases, and old bottles are silhouetted against the walls and windows. Of particular significance is the J. Cheney Wells collection of glass paper weights, which have been gathered from the far corners of Europe and America.

THE HARRINGTON GUN SHOP is another gambrel-roofed house, inspired by an 18th century dwelling in Brookfield, Massachusetts. It contains a remarkable collection of firearms, swords, locks, and weighing devices. It has a pitch-roofed ell which shelters, in addition to a replica of an old gunsmith's forge, an amusing exhibit of a hundred or more homemade rat traps.

Gun collectors will find much to interest them in the front room of the Harrington Gun Shop. Decoy ducks, drums, and military headgear all seem at home in these surroundings.

A rear exhibition room is largely given over to the seamier side of the world of firearms — policemen's billys, skeleton keys, handcuffs, leg irons and padlocks. Only a good gruesome garotte is missing.

THE HITCHCOCK BOOT SHOP makes a dramatic red-and-white sihouette against the winter sky. This small one-room building has two doors and ten windows, making the shop as cheerful as it is quaint.

The interior of the Hitchcock Boot Shop has been fitted out with all the tools, benches, and forms which might have been used by an old-time cobbler. The shop is named for one in nearby Brimfield.

THE WOOD WORKING MUSEUM

This colorful structure dates from the early 19th century, and probably served as a shop on the original David Wight farm. The peculiar design of its off-center front door is explained by the fact that it came originally from a corner cupboard. The building contains an instructive collection of early wood working tools and equipment.

The thoroughness of the Wood Working Museum may be judged by this well populated rack of old fashioned wooden planes.

The sunlight pours in on the venerable carpenter's bench at the far end of the Wood Working Museum. The studied disarray of the exhibit gives the illusion that the old wood worker has just stepped out to lunch. The white-washed front portion of the museum displays the tools of the housewright, cabinetmaker, and cooper.

THE WEAVE SHOP

One of the most important and applauded phases of Old Sturbridge Village is its Craft Program. From the outset its aim has been to pay a tribute to the skill and ingenuity of the early settlers, not only by assembling in one area their houses, their church, their stores, workshops, schools and taverns, but by bringing their occupations to life. Vitality has been injected into this picture of early American enterprise by a group of skilled craftsmen who produce textiles, pottery, cabinet work, woodenware, metal work, and a variety of worthwhile articles in the tradition of their ancestors. These craftsmen give demonstrations and lessons, but they also produce objects for sale and use. It is a self supporting project, and one which is particularly acclaimed by visitors, especially the school children.

The Weave Shop, as an example, contains spinning wheels, an ancient loom, and implements for working flax and wool. But interest centers on the skillful young lady who threads her shuttle back and forth on a highly functional loom. She gives lessons, produces handsome fabrics, and annually answers the eager questions of an incredible number of visitors, young and old.

THE WOOD TURNER'S SHOP

In the background of this summer vista are the Weave Shop and, at the right, the neat rectangular building which houses a skilled wood turner. On a modern lathe he turns out finely grained wooden plates, and from mahogany blocks he chisels out salad bowls. Another specialty is a pine utility board, which handsomely befits a slab of seasoned coon cheese.

THE CABINET SHOP, shown at the right, is the largest of the craft buildings. Under its broad roof cabinetmakers and a skilled furniture finisher ply their trades — and answer questions.

A wood turner fashions legs for a traditional New England bedstead at this modern lathe.

A veteran cabinetmaker demonstrates the subtler points of finishing a classic wall table.

An exhibition of old copper kettles, pots, pans and measures lend atmosphere and well burnished color to the METAL SHOP. Seated before a work table contrived from a massive stubby log, the metalsmith raises a metal bowl with the same tools that have been used in New England for generations.

THE POTTERY SHOP

At the far edge of the village a commodious, well-equipped shop has been set up for the display of old and modern pottery, and for the manufacture of modern pieces in time-proven techniques. A blend of youthful enthusiasm and traditional quality is expressed in this original grouping in the display room.

Visitors never tire of watching this deft young lady raise a piece of clay into a graceful dish.

On an idyllic midsummer day, Old Sturbridge Village has an indefinably poignant appeal. What could be more gracious than the little Mashapaug Cottage, serene besides its towering elm on a July afternoon?

THE CARETAKER'S HOUSE is a cheerful little gambrel-roofed affair, with a porch set into its ell, and and impressive vegetable garden in the back. It is an adaptation of an early house in Sturbridge.

As a farewell glimpse, it seems appropriate to choose the first building to appear on these rolling acres now dedicated to Old Sturbridge Village. When David Wight II built his story-and-a-half cottage here in 1783, he could not foresee the extraordinary series of events which were to follow. First he had the rare fortune to win $5,000 in a Harvard College lottery. With that stroke of luck, he moved this pitch-roofed cottage away from the site and on it built himself the most imposing mansion in the region. He could not anticipate that his mansion would later burn to the ground. Least of all could he divine that a retired manufacturer from Southbridge would move his old cottage back to its original setting, and make it a part of Old Sturbridge Village, an adventure in Americanism which will leave its indelible imprint on everyone who has the good fortune to pass along the Old Bay Path.

INDEX

AMERICAN OPTICAL SHOP	56	MEETING HOUSE	36
BLACKSMITH'S HOUSE	14	METAL SHOP	65
BLACKSMITH'S SHOP	16	CHENEY SAW-MILL	8
BLACKSMITH'S WAGON SHED	18	WIGHT GRIST MILL	10
CABINET SHOP	64	MILL POND	8
CARETAKER'S HOUSE	67	MILLER'S HOUSE	13
DENESON SCHOOL HOUSE	46	POTTERY SHOP	66
FENNO HOUSE	39	QUINEBAUG RIVER	7
STEPHEN FITCH HOUSE	40	SOLOMON RICHARDSON HOUSE	27
GEBHARD BARN	19	TAVERN	20
GRANT'S GENERAL STORE	47	TIN SHOP	55
HARRINGTON GUN SHOP	57	WEAVE SHOP	62
HITCHCOCK SHOE SHOP	59	DAVID WIGHT COTTAGE	68
MANSION HOUSE	54	OLIVER WIGHT HOUSE	3
MASHAPAUG COTTAGE	67	WOOD TURNER'S SHOP	63
MASHAPAUG HOUSE	33	WOOD WORKING TOOLS MUSEUM	60